SWINGING WITH GAR

by Gar Witherspoon

ISBN 0-9618178-0-1

Introduction

They say there are only eight plots to a play and what seems like more are variations thereof. Golf has been around some 300 years now, and a great number of books have been written on the subject. What makes this book different from any other? In one area I call it the difference between the saying and the doing. Many players say one thing and do it differently themselves. Everything in this book is exactly the way the author plays the game.

There is a saying: "What's in the mind is intellectual; what comes out is ineffectual." By this I mean, what's in the muscle memory or the computer bank of one's body does not always come out in the telling or the way one teaches. In other words, some people have the ability within themselves but they are not able to translate it over to a student.

There is another saying: "If you steal from one it's plagiarism; if you steal from many it's research." Having had lessons from over 200 golf professionals in several western states over the years as I have traveled, it has given me an opportunity to take lessons with many approaches and study the methods of all types of teachers. During 40 years of playing and 18 years of teaching I have been able to sift out the wheat from the chaff and put down the theory of the swing in my own individual way.

I have found in over 18 years of teaching, at one period 24 lessons a day, six days a week for nine years, that the light of understanding does not go on in everyone at the same time. A good teacher, therefore, must be able to say things in different ways, or if you will, present material from many different angles in order for the person to understand and then translate the moving pieces into a consistent swing. Thus, I am not a carbon copy of any one teacher or professional. As my golf evolution has been a potpourri of ingredients which have led to an unusual bisecting of the golf swing and close game, and having spent years as a teacher without the pressures of tour playing or club management, I have put on blinders, focusing in on countless types of golf enthusiasts.

The cause and effect relationship of failure to success and mediocrity to fame have been carefully studied so that what follows is a practical approach to teaching golf which takes years off the learning curve and presents the subject in a concise and experienced manner. The plot of the play is not different; however, the method of telling the story offers a new and fresh approach to an old story. Let's say the character in this play will wear a different costume and project a unique voice. This is not an encyclopedia of golf that is covering the subject from A to Z like the history of golf or the history of the ball or the history of the club or golf course construction, nor am I going to cover the rules of golf. This has been done in a fine book called *New Rules of Golf* by Tom Watson, an official publication of the United States Golf Association.

This book is dedicated to Floyd Sparks and my wife Lois, both of whom provided the enthusiasm and support which made this book possible.

TABLE OF CONTENTS

CHAPTER 1

THE THEORY OF GOLF

Golf is not difficult to learn. Golf is difficult to learn to play well. Golf is one sport where we are trying to get the lowest score possible. In other sports, such as football, basketball, baseball, we're attempting to get a high score.

Golf is a game using a ball and a club. The goal is to get the ball, whose diameter is 1.68 inches into a 4¼ inch hole. The distance we are attempting to accomplish this feat in varies from a few inches from the hole to several hundred yards from the hole in as few strokes as possible. In addition, we carry an arsenal of 14 weapons called clubs to hit our targets.

A regulation golf course averages 72 strokes to play the game from start to finish for 18 holes. The national average is 112 strokes approximately, and if one plays in the 90s, they're in the top ten percent of the nation. If they play in the 80s, they're in the top five percent in the nation.

There are approximately 300 touring professionals making their living playing golf. Only a hundred of these make approximately $25,000 or more per year. There are also club professionals who make their living running golf courses with concessions like golf cart rentals and pro shops specializing in golf equipment and attire.

Another classification of a golf professional is the teaching professional who specializes in transferring his knowledge and ability to his students. This is the author's area of expertise, so for the next 18 chapters we will unfold the story as to why the golf swing is difficult when it is played at its best. The best is going to be our goal. I define the golf swing as the ability to move the clubhead down a target line with proper speed and under control for as long and as straight as possible. We are going to try to build our swings within our physical abilities, taking into account the amount of time we have to practice and our desire, which is the ultimate umbrella held over our entire game. So we must start with the desire to learn and improve the game.

The game of golf dates back to the 1600s, and when it first started in Scotland there were a mere handful of rules. As it has grown, and as the engineering and technology has come along over the last 300 years, we have seen drastic changes in clubs, in ball design, in golf courses, and of course, in the amount of rules under which we play.

We are going to talk briefly about why the game is difficult to play at its best, but we're going to start with some information covered thoroughly in Chapter 7. That foundation is called the grip, and we will look at our development as though we are going to build a puzzle. We will put the pieces together, and at the end we'll create a picture. If we don't take too big a bite at one time, we will not choke on our uphill challenge to build the proper golf swing.

Now we're going to discuss procedure before we get into some of the reasons why golf is difficult. This means that for every cause there is an effect.

There is a reason why we do everything in golf. If there's not a reason we either should not be doing it or we don't understand it. In having audited over 200 golf professionals over the last 40 years, I have found that one of the weaknesses in proper teaching is in not making the student understand why we do something, and more importantly, in his own individual case, how he can correct those things that he's doing wrong. A student should not stand and slice a ball, scratch his head and say, "I don't know why I did that." He should be able to say, "Oh, I swung inside," or "I opened my club face," or "I supinated my hands," or whatever. And remember, each individual has his own particular golf swing, just like a finger print, which will not relate to the person next to him.

The basic swing and its characteristics will be the same as far as teaching and building what I call our mechanical man. The individuality of the person will come out even though the ball lands in the same place as another person's, and the score is approximately the same, but the route by which we get there may vary considerably from person to person. So we're going to build a procedure where each part is connected like the old thigh bone to the hip bone, and so forth. We're going to build each piece and connect it together and overlay it with timing, tempo and rhythm.

But before we do that, back to some of the reasons why golf is difficult. We have a very small ball and we have a very large swing arc. The swing arc is the path that the club takes as it moves through the nine positions of the swing which we will be covering in later chapters.

We have a bag full of clubs; legally we may carry 14. There's no rule as to what those clubs need to be. The average touring pro will carry a 1 through 9-iron, two wedges, a putter, and two woods. They may be mixed up into different numbers, but the total must be no more than 14.

We have, therefore, as will be covered in Chapter 4 extensively, the internal struggle or the psychology of golf, because it's not good enough just to be able to build a repeating and consistent swing. We must have the right frame of mind and learn to relax when we go out on the golf course in order to use less strength and more finesse. So, as a general term, we can say that golf is not a game of strength; it is a game of generating clubhead speed which leads us to compressing the ball off the club face. That will be covered quite a bit in Chapter 5.

Contributing to the game's difficulty is the engineering, or the different parts of a club. There are six of these which we are going to talk about in Chapter 3; these give us variables. That is, the grip may be changed; the shaft may be changed; the length may be changed. So we have decisions in that area which make it a little bit difficult. The golf course itself creates a formidable opponent in that it offers varying conditions such as long and short grass, bunkers, water hazards, to say nothing of nature's impediments such as wind, rain and even snow.

We also have an opponent that challenges us differently on any given day. The thing I like about golf is that it is a personal thing. We are really playing against ourself. Golf is not considered a team sport like basketball and football. However, there are a number of games that we can play with teams and different ways that we can play in foursomes and with couples, but in the most universally played method called stroke play, which is the lowest strokes that you can score on the golf course, it's really us against the course. So then, when a person cheats or kicks the ball forward, or changes his score when no one is looking, he really isn't hurting anyone but himself. Golf is the ultimate challenge of man against himself and man against the course.

The golfer is never satisfied with the score. There have been professionals interviewed on television who have shot 68s, for example, and one of those professionals said, "one day, maybe, I'll put it all together." Pressure is not a golfer's best friend. On any given day a good golfer can score well, but his mental attitude and the pressure under which he is playing is the razor's edge. We'll talk quite a bit more about that in Chapter 4, The Internal Struggle.

Golf is a game of habit, of patterns and reflexes. If I were to ask you to stand in front of me a few feet away and I threw a golf ball at you, you would reach up automatically for the ball. This probably started when you picked up your first rattle. Reflex, then, is something that happens as it has been conditioned in the body through constant repetition which later comes out automatically. The brain thinks more slowly than our muscle reflexes as we swing a golf club, so we're not able to think our way through a golf swing. We must, therefore, memorize the moves piece-by-piece and step-by-step. We call this muscle memory.

A touring pro in one year of practice and playing may hit between 100,000 and 300,000 balls in order to keep this muscle memory in his computer bank. One of my basic philosophies is that the ball gets in the way of the swing. This is very important because I have spent many years teaching golf in classrooms and one of the questions my students ask first is: "how can we learn without a golf ball," and I tell them that if they cannot stand up in front of me and make a decent golf swing, then, when they put the ball in front of the clubhead they're going to become intimidated because the little golf ball intimidates people because they're always trying to strike it too hard.

The golf swing has too many moving parts for the average person to control. If we go into advanced golf there are some 27 parts to the swing. So we cannot think of more than one, or at best two things at a time when we're practicing or moving in the golf swing. We need to think, as we build the golf swing, that we have a barrel of faults; we're going to gradually take out and throw away as many faults as possible. The more faults we can eliminate from the barrel, the lower our score will be, and the better we will improve. We are all creatures of habit.

As most people are right-handed, or as many left-handed persons convert to what we call a right-handed stance, we need to know why we have problems hitting the ball with our strong right side and why golf has been called a left-sided game. This was never adequately explained to me as I went through my years of training in golf, so I'm going to explain it in a way that's a little bit different, but I think it will help you understand why we call golf a left-sided sport, in other words, pulling left instead of pushing right.

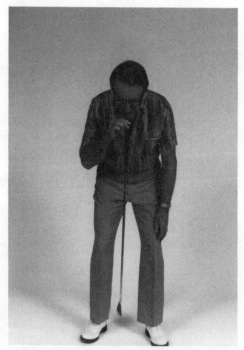

Photograph 1.

Let's look at Photographs 1, 2 and 3. The first photograph shows the club hanging straight down from the chin as though it were a plumb line. The chin, therefore, is the center of the golf swing. We will put the ball in the

Photograph 2.

center or in line with the chin equally between the feet; this is the bottom of our swing arc. In Photograph 2 you will note that the club is hanging straight down from the right shoulder or in line with the right foot. If I simply stand in place and swing the club into the ground from about half way up, I would strike the ground behind the ball and close to my right foot. This is called right-hand domination and pushing or shoving. We can also call it chopping.

In Photograph 3, by moving the club in line with the left shoulder and letting it hang down, it is in line with the left foot. By pulling the club with the left shoulder, arm and hand, I will strike the ground in front of the ball four to six inches. If I also move the rest of my body by turning my hips and moving left with the knees, I will keep the club down the target line long and straight and I will hit through the ball instead of at the ball. So we never say, "Oh, there's a golf ball. I'm going to hit it." We always think of hitting through the ball. This will be covered more in Chapter 8 on alignment.

What we're trying to do is break our instinctive right-sidedness as creatures of habit the way we would pick up a hammer or write or one of the hundreds of things we do with the right hand. We must, therefore, get rid of this type of feeling as soon as we step on the golf course and have another person evolve which uses different parts of the body than we use in our everyday habits.

Photograph 3.

In addition to overcoming right-side domination, we must learn to overcome the instinct to look. By this I mean looking where the ball is going and not where it's been. In sports we're used to playing and watching. The ball normally flies toward us, is kicked at us, is hit toward us, but in golf, the ball remains stationary until we strike it away from us.

Now, this is one nice thing about the golf game. We can go through our basic setup that we will call fixed parts: the grip, the stance, the posture, and the alignment without fear of the ball flying at us by another player from some other location. So in this portion of our work, we can take our time; we can practice and rehearse before we strike the ball. This is the bright side of what we're doing. We're going to break our work down as we go through the next few chapters into fixed, or non-moving parts, and moving parts. Everything from these two categories is a takeoff, and as we go through the chapters, they will be defined to us in detail.

CHAPTER 2

THE BALL

The golf ball is a sphere like the earth, which means that it has an equator. If we hit above the equator, or strike the ball in that location with our club, the ball will not get airborne. So, in order to make the golf ball fly upward, we must hit below the equator. The ideal place for a medium handicap and high handicap or a beginning golfer to strike the ball is underneath by cutting the grass down to the dirt so that it flies up in the air. But at this stage, that type of golfer should not worry about taking a big divot or cutting an amount of dirt under the ball or in front of it. You can play a very good game of golf by cutting the grass and watching it jump up as if you cut it with clippers, and don't worry about going too deeply into the ground. Now, if we hit behind the golf ball, it is called "fat," and if we hit above center, it's called "topping." If we hit below center, but above the ground, we call it "thin."

A golf ball must have direction in order to control it and allow the air to direct the ball either right, left or straight. The guiding system is the dimples and with the new modern technology we have in computers, different manufacturers have different configurations of dimples and different numbers; the average is running about 365 dimples on a ball. The figure can run into the 350 area or up into the 400s. These dimples are like the rudder on a boat, or the wings on an airplane, both of which give direction. Without the dimples there would be no direction and the ball could slide in any unpredicted direction.

A golf ball is 1.68 inches in diameter, which makes it approximately an inch and a half. It weighs 1.62 ounces. There are about ten balls to the pound, therefore, our golf club is approximately eight times heavier than the ball. A 150 pound person is 1500 times heavier than a ball. In some sports, this proportion of body weight to sphere is completely different. One example would be bowling. With a 16 pound ball, a 160 pound man is only ten times heavier than the object he is trying to propel. So we have enough mass in the club and a great deal more mass in the body to be able to successfully propel the golf ball. So what we are really after is clubhead speed. Clubhead speed gives us distance.

We have another factor in a golf ball called compression. There are three basic types of compression factors in a golf ball. If a ball has a red name and red letters, it will be an 80 compression ball. This is considered a woman's ball. If the ball has a black name and red letters, it is a 90 compression ball. This is the average ball that most people play with and close to 80 percent of the golf pros also play with this ball. The 100 compression ball has black letters and black numbers.

Now if we did a stop action picture of a golf ball, it would show the ball flattened or compressed on the club face. So we can look at two golfers that might swing identically, but one would have a completely different type of reaction on the golf ball. It would have a zing and fly through the air much further because that golfer has reached a level of clubhead speed to give compression. This would be like launching a rocket and adding a booster rocket to it to go into orbit. The faster the clubhead, the more compression and distance we will get.

Without going back through history when the golf ball was first made out of leather and stuffed with feathers, we need to mention that there are two basic types of golf balls. Some have a small rubber ball in the center wrapped with rubber bands and then finished with a cover. That's called a three-piece ball, and then a two-piece ball which has a solid core and a surlyn cover which is a cut-resistant Dupont product. Most people are playing with a two-piece ball because of its cut-resistant characteristics. Any major name-brand golf ball in this day and age is well-made and will cover a distance great enough to accommodate the average golfer.

I would like to cover the ball positions for each club in your bag. We will assume now that we have our feet approximately shoulder width apart and our toes touching a straight line. The center will be the chin line, as discussed earlier, the line achieved by touching a club to our chin and letting it hang straight down like a surveyor's plumb line. This we do with the 5, 6, 7, 8 and 9-irons and the pitching wedge. The mid-irons are the 5, 6, 7-irons; the short irons are the 8 and 9, and I'm going to add the pitching wedge, if it's played in a full swing. These six clubs play the ball centered.

The 2, 3, 4-irons, called the long irons, play the ball three inches left of center. The 2, 3, 4 and 5-woods play the ball in the same position, three inches left of center. With these seven clubs we can also relate it to three inches from the left heel. If we laid a club down so that the toe of the club touched our left heel and laid it straight out in front of us from the heel, that would be three inches to the right of the left heel. You will notice that particular position in Photograph 4. Also the three ball positions are in Photograph 5.

The ball played off the heel is used when we play or stroke the ball with the driver. At this point we could tee up the ball and we can see that it would be struck on the upswing past the bottom of our swing arch which is in the center. If the 2, 3, 4 and 5-woods are played as a driver or used as our first shot off a tee or teeing area, the ball would then be played in the same position as would the driver, which is also called the No. 1 wood. When we tee up an iron on the teeing area, which is the first stroke on a hole, we tee

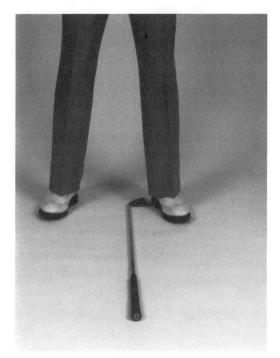

Photograph 4.

the ball up in its normal position either center or three inches to the left of center. The proper way to tee up the ball is to place it on a tee just slightly above the grass to give us a nice lie, which is the easiest way for us to hit the ball.

The teeing area, which I have been talking about, is made up of a rectangular box between the two tee markers and up to two club lengths behind. The ball must be within that area to eliminate a penalty; however, the feet may be outside of the teeing area. I prefer to stand back about one club length behind the tees because as the day wears on, most golfers stand between the tee markers and chew up the grass when they strike the ball and with the spikes in their shoes. By moving back slightly and to the right or to the left to help get the proper angle, we have better grass to stand on and better grass on which to place the ball.

In chipping and pitching, which will be discussed in later chapters, we play the ball center. On putting and sand traps, also discussed later, we play the ball off or in line with our left heel.

I would like to come back for a moment to the proper way we should tee up a golf ball when using the driver or the fairway woods as the driver. When

Photograph 5.

we place the ball on a tee, half of the ball should be above the top of the club face. If we tee it higher than this, it would tend to fly too high, and if we tee it lower than this, we would have trouble getting the ball airborne.

CHAPTER 3

THE CLUB

You may carry 14 golf clubs in your bag. If you carry more, it is not legal according to the rules of golf. You can carry 14 putters or 14 drivers. The rules don't say what you have to put in your bag. Most golf professionals carry the 1 through 9-irons, two wedges, one putter, and two woods. Most amateurs carry the 2 through 9-irons, two wedges, a putter, and three woods, either the 1, 3 and 5-woods or the 1, 3, 4-woods. This gives us an arsenal of 14 weapons to hit our targets. The choice of these weapons or clubs is what makes the game of golf a challenge in order to pick the right club to hit the right distance.

I would like to break down several of the variables of the golf clubs and explain a little bit about what parts of the club may be changed to fit the individual. Generally it relates to the length of arms, or how tall or how short one is.

The first of these variables is the overall weight or the club weight. This is usually standard as manufactured or engineered and most of the time this weight, 12 to 14 ounces, is not changed. The swing weight, however, is the weight placed at the club head and may be changed and in this area we have choices.

There is a scale that's kept in most golf shops whereby the club may be inserted into the scale and the weight at the head weighed. Generally anything in the C range, up to C-9, is in the women's weight area. And D-0 through D-6 or 7 is in the men's range. Most golf professionals play with a D-2 swing weight. Many older golfers prefer to go down to a D-1 or a D-0, sometimes even into the women's part of the scale. The average woman will play with a C-4, C-5 or C-6. This is an area where the golf professional with whom you work can give you some advice based on your personal swing, size and your weight.

The shaft of the club can vary in different flexes. They come in regular, stiff, extra stiff and flex. Some companies number them one, two, three and four. Most golfers play with a regular stiffness or flex shaft. The better golfers will go for a stiffer shaft, and most women play with a flex shaft.

The grip may be built up by having a professional take it off the shaft, wrap additional tape around it and place it back on so that it's actually larger in diameter for a person with larger hands. The club or grip may also be lengthened. For example, one-half inch over length or three-quarters or even one inch if a person needs a longer club. This is done by taking the grip off and placing a plug into the shaft, replacing the grip and adding an over-length. Very few people play with an under-length, but it is possible to cut a club down for a younger person, a junior or a short person.

There are other parts of the club that are also necessary to know. The cap is that end of the grip that touches the floor when the club is inverted; this term will also be discussed later. The shaft varies in length one-half inch from its neighbor. So then, if we take a mid-range club like a 5-iron, the 6-iron would be one-half inch shorter and the 4-iron would be one-half inch longer. The head of the club is like our foot, with a toe, a heel and a sole.

The score marks on the face of a club are designed to impart a back spin on the ball as it climbs up the face and is projected forward with underspin. These score marks should be kept clean by wiping the club between shots and cleaning the clubs with a soft brush and water after each round.

The pitch or the loft of the club face is engineered in degrees so that each iron varies three degrees from its neighbor and for each wood, four degrees. The flattest club in your bag is a putter with zero degrees in order to roll the ball. The next flattest is the driver with some 12 to 14 degrees loft. The pitching wedge is approximately two lofts or eight degrees from the 9-iron, so this is a very important club to have in your bag.

These different degrees of loft or pitch to the club face, which are standard in all clubs, translates to a different distance as we pick the club for the number of yards we wish to travel. If we start with a 5-iron, and use a standard distance of 150 yards, the 4-iron would translate to 160 yards; the 3-iron, 170 yards; the 2-iron, 180 yards; the 5-wood, 190 yards; the 4-wood, 200 yards; the 3-wood, 210 yards; the 2-wood, 220 yards; and the driver, 230 yards.

Coming back and going shorter, the 6-iron would hit 140 yards, the 7, 130, the 8, 120, and the 9-iron, 110. Now these are standard lengths for a good golfer using the full swing with all the basic clubs. It would be advisable for you to take a 3 x 5 index card and graph your own swing. In other words, start with a 5-iron. If you hit the 5-iron 130 yards, then extend out in each direction on that card the distances in which you would use your other clubs.

The clubs allow a distance of ten yards apart. So when you first graph your swing you can carry this 3 x 5 card with you and as your numbers change you can write in the new distances as your game improves. So the figures I gave you are fairly tough distances to reach if you're a beginning or high handicap golfer, so I put it in here only as a goal for you to try to reach.

You will notice that as the numbers of the clubs go down, the distances get greater, and as the numbers go up, the distances get shorter. Now you can see by this graph covering the full swing that we have an area which has not been covered. This gray area from 110 yards into the green will be covered with specialty shots called chipping, high pitch, low pitch and putting. These will be covered later.

The most important thing to understand in this chapter on the club is that the swing is the same for all clubs. The only thing that changes is the ball position as covered in Chapter 2, and the distance that we stand from the ball, which is determined by the length of the shaft of the club we are holding, so we will learn to vary the distance from the ball as we gain experience. The ball should always be placed in the center of the club face as we ground the club and prepare to strike the ball.

There's one other part of the club that's important to know and that is the hosel which is from the heel of the club up to and connecting the shaft to the head. We'll talk about this more when we talk about the diseases of golf, but this hosel can be an area on which we strike the ball and in turn direct it sharply to the right.

We should think of ourselves as a mechanical person. Over the next few chapters we are going to build a mechanical man or a mechanical woman. This would relate to parts of a drill. The "chuck" is a mechanical device for holding drills and the "bit" is a drilling part, so we will become the chuck and the bits will become the clubs. If we stood, with the proper degree of knee bend and back bend, and someone kept handing us clubs and adjusting the ball for the length for us, we should ideally hit a ball down the straight line ten yards apart as we add the clubs into our chuck. The only time we would vary our swing is when we are working with less than a full swing, that is a quarter swing, half swing, three-quarter swing and the specialty shots of chipping, pitching and putting.

Because our clubs vary one-half inch in length difference between its neighbor, each club will give us a different size swing arc, which is nothing more than the path the clubhead travels in a circle. We will consider our head as the center of the circle and our arms as the spokes of that wheel. As the swing arc changes, we will have other variables which will come into play and vary slightly; that is, the timing, the tempo and the rhythm, but our mechanical man will continue to move the same way each time we swing.

Because of the engineering in the pitch or loft of the club face, we will have different trajectories in the flight of the ball. As the club gets shorter and the number larger, like with a 9-iron, the ball will fly higher. As we get lower in number, like the 2-iron, the club has less pitch and the ball will fly lower. If we place a ball behind a normal position for which it is intended, it will fly lower. If we place it further forward of the normal position for which it's intended, it will fly higher.

Trajectory is a difficult thing to describe. It is something we learn to visually understand as we work on our golf game and particularly when we work with a qualified instructor. Nevertheless, proper trajectory is very important as it relates to the body movement into the backswing. This will be discussed more in Chapter 6, The Diseases.

Before closing this chapter we have one other important part of the nomenclature of a club and that is called the "lie." If we had a correctly fitted club, and we took our address position with our knees bent and back bent, our correct arm position preparing to hit the ball, we should be able to slide a piece of paper under the sole of the club and have it stop equally between the toe and the heel. An upright stance of the club that is not of the correct length would stand more on its toe. As we struck the ball and the ground, the toe would dig in and cause the club to spin out and send the ball generally to the right.

The other end of the scale would be a very short person or a person who bends over abnormally and rests the heel on the ground so that the club sticks up and we have much less of the club face with which to strike the ball. Here again we have a variable in the club that can be corrected by bending the club slightly at the hosel. This should be done under the assistance of a golf pro. But it is an important area to give us the maximum amount of club face on the ball without being too flat or too upright.

CHAPTER 4

THE INTERNAL STRUGGLE

The internal struggle concerns the preparations of the inner person for playing golf. It is not as much a psyching up to get the adrenaline going, but an understanding of what's to come and how to prepare for it. It is more mental than psychological. On any given day two golf professionals, for example, having the same mechanical man, moving the same way would only have a difference of mental attitude. Their mental preparedness would give one or the other the razor's edge. Therefore there is the "off-golf-course-you" and the "on-golf-course-you." You may drive to the golf course holding your steering wheel with white fingers because you are tensed or unrelaxed about going to play the game. In this chapter I'm going to give you information on some of the things that will help you to change into the "on-golf-course-you" and some specific mental exercises which will help you become relaxed when you step up to the tee.

This chapter is put in at this point because from here on we're going to physically be working on the actions and parts of the swing, the faults, the cures, the exercises, the drills, the timing, tempo and rhythm. So, in addition to preparing us to play the game of golf with the right attitude, this chapter is placed here to prepare us for what is to come.

When we are tense we tend to swing too hard. The single most important problem that a golfer faces is the tendency to be too strong, too tense, and too disjointed in a swing, so we need to practice relaxing. These five exercises can help you in other parts of your daily activity when you're called to do things that make you tense, or they may even help you to go to sleep more quickly.

The first example is to think of yourself as a glass person. Hollow through whom you may see. You take this glass person, which in your mind is in your own image and fill it up with a colored liquid. It may be blue or green; however, I prefer to use red. That's just my own personal color I use in my glass man as I fill him up to the top. Once you have your glass person filled with the color liquid of your choice, stand in a relaxed upright position and allow the liquid in your mind to run from your head down through your body as it empties through your feet and makes a puddle on the ground. You should close your eyes while doing this and you will visually see that the liquid is going down until you become clear and transparent. The cleaner that you can imagine this glass man as being, in other words, without spots, as though you used a dishwashing soap that left you spotless, it will tend to help you in this kind of exercise.

With the number two exercise you can imagine you are a blanket that someone has picked up and walked over and dropped in a corner. You feel yourself as the blanket falling into a heap and relaxing totally.

In exercise three imagine you are a puppet. Someone is holding the strings above you that you cannot see. The puppeteer relaxes one hand, the other hand, the elbow, the head, the knees, and gradually releases the tension on the strings. This exercise can effectively be done by sitting down or seated in your car as you park in the golf course lot. So you ultimately, then, let everything slump and relax and your neck drop so that your chin is resting close to your chest and you feel this relaxation throughout your body.

Imagine that you're a life-size balloon for exercise four. I like to think of my balloon as being a caricature of the way I look. It's better if you draw a direct relationship to yourself rather than just thinking of a pretty colored balloon. I blow up this balloon and gradually let the air out through my feet, and I close my eyes and physically see myself collapsing so that when I get through, I am collapsed, lying on the ground just as if we had let the air out of any other type of balloon, and when it's finished, it's totally empty.

The one I particularly like is number five. This one you can do sitting, lying down or standing. I generally do it when I'm seated. I imagine that I am a person made of concrete. I am very, very heavy. As I sit in my chair I am so heavy that I feel myself sliding down through the chair, breaking the bottom of the chair with my weight. I then continue downward beginning to break and splinter the floor and start to fall through. At this point I have six of my friends (you can use any number that you wish in this exercise) come in and try, before I fall through the floor, to reach down and lift me back up. I am so heavy because I am made of concrete that they are having trouble holding me, so I gradually begin to slip away.

These five exercises, if you do them constantly, will put you in an extremely relaxed mode. I have done these for years and have cut the time down to the point where I can do them all in my head in a minute or two and be totally relaxed. This type of an exercise can be done before you speak publicly, before you ask your boss for a raise, and as I said earlier, before you go to bed. After some 20 years of doing this type of mental relaxation, I can put myself in the proper on-golf-course attitude.

Another thing that will help you in your internal struggle to prepare for playing the game of golf is to understand that when we stand too long we become tense. There is a term in golf called a "waggle," and most golfers have their own form of this, but in essence when we address the ball, it's a movement from the wrist, taking the club back in short strokes to keep us moving and keep the muscles from tightening up. It will also help you to overcome standing too long by making some decisions ahead of time, before you come up to address the ball. For example, you should have your club, if it's a standard shot without any particular difficulties to it, picked out as you walk up to the ball. If it's 150 yards from the green, you may just pick your 5-iron out and have it prepared. Also you should have your line in mind when you walk up to the ball. I always look for something that's about a foot in front of the ball. This could be a bent twig, a pebble, a piece of grass, a leaf or what have you, but as I walk up, I line up this gunsight to my target, and as I address the ball, I place my feet, my knees, my hips and shoulders parallel to this line.

For those of you that are bowlers, you will have heard of the term "spot bowling," which means that we throw our bowling ball over an arrow at the early part of the lane so that we don't concentrate clear down at the end or at the pins. The same thing is true here. If you pick the right club and have a line which you can get parallel to, you also have a shorter target over which you pass the club. So, at this point I do not look beyond my gunsight, just a foot or so in front of the ball toward the target. I simply concentrate on taking my club straight over that line because at that point the ball will have become airborne.

We need to know that we become overcautious when we are afraid of failure. This is a tendency that goes into many other parts of our life. Overcautiousness in a lot of sports, for example, football, when the clock is running down and the team is leading, sometimes leads to failure. Now you say why do I need to worry about the psychological problem of being overcautious on the golf course. Well, the golf course is not really a safe place because we have such things as hitting over water, bunkers, sidehill lies, wind, and so on. I'm not suggesting that we not play the percentages. A good golfer will work within the framework of his ability and not take chances. There are times, however, when we must go to the outside of our ability scale and take a chance that has a less than 100 percent chance of success.

We have another problem on the golf course which is called "vague fear." Psychologists tell us that it is harder for us as individuals to stand "vague fear" and that we can tolerate more easily "known fear." This comes in all types of situations where people are in the unknown and are in constant fear because there isn't anything or any direction they can take by knowing what's going on. This, of course, translates to the point that there is no safety of a golf course because of our choices, club selection, and all the things I've mentioned earlier until we have built an extreme confidence and until then we do not get out or away from this vague fear problem. But by knowing that it exists, and that it will become less and less of a problem, it helps equip us in understanding how the inner-self works on the golf course.

One of our biggest problems on the golf course is anger. Anger causes brute strength, which is fine for football, or chopping a tree, or picking up a heavy weight. But when we're working with a very light ball and a club that is less than a pound, we cannot afford to get angry because our golf club turns into a sledge hammer.

The slow pace of golf gives us too much time to think. The several minutes between shots gives us time for excessive study. For example, when you walk down stairs you don't think. It is a good idea, if we don't have a difficult shot which requires a lot of preparation as we walk to the ball, to think momentarily about something else. As it were, to put our mind on other things so that we don't get more tense as we walk to the ball because of the slow pace. A little joking or a little thinking of things on a lighter side may be of help, as long as we know that this particular problem in golf conflicts with our inner man because we seem to operate better if we move in a quicker pace.

Golf is a paradox. If seems easy when you don't know better. We've all heard people say, "I don't see why you go out there and chase that little white ball around the golf course," or "that doesn't look very difficult to me because when I watched it on television the fellows make it look easy, and the shots always come out in pretty good shape." But as with all professionals and whatever endeavor they're involved in, whether it be piano, or sports, or art, because of long years of practice in doing what they do, it seems easy. So then, when we get out and actually take up golf or play it, we're able to fail more easily because we have conflict and tension due to the fact that our psyche thinks that we're doing something that's very easy. We can put this in the category of reverse psychology by saying, "oh, that isn't very tough," but when we do it and fail, then we have tension.

At this point we have another little exercise I call "shaking-the-tension-out-of-the-arms" where if you feel that you're uneasy and in conflict, you can simply put the club down and shake your arms and hands and fingers in a very loose fashion and feel the tension just shaking out of your hands. I find this particularly helpful in the right hand, which is definitely the arm and hand I do not want to tighten up.

By having 14 clubs to choose from, we're constantly faced with choices. Many people do better when they don't have so many choices, and as we say, we make it easier on ourselves if we can reduce the choices we have to make in life. But now we have 14 golf clubs. This takes us into the area of vague fear and something seeming easier than it is which might lead to anger. So in your practice sessions, and as you graph your swings on a 3 x 5 card, you will build confidence in your choice and feel that you've picked up the right club without looking back with a question as to "Have I done the right thing?" There is a saying, "a weak man blames others for his shortcomings. A strong man looks to himself and becomes stronger."

Therefore, we never want to allow negative thoughts to creep into our inner-self, as these will gradually grow and harvest unsuccessful golf games. We want to plant seeds of success and always think positively. If we start this early on, like forgetting a bad shot and going on and thinking about the next one, we create the habit pattern so that the inner struggle becomes less and less, and on the other side of the balance scale, our confidence increases and outweighs the items that I have just covered. Do not diminish the importance of this chapter on preparing ourselves mentally to play golf.

CHAPTER 5

THE PHYSICS LAWS

The formula for energy in golf is $\dfrac{MV^2}{2} = E$ (Golf)

$$V^2 = E \text{ (Wind)}$$

This formula translates to mass times velocity squared divided by two equals energy. In this formula we will call E clubhead speed. If we were to take a golf tee and simply drop it as we were going to drop a golf ball, that would be called the "Law of Inertia." If we picked up the tee and flipped it with our finger out away from our body, we could probably project the tee about five yards. This flipping is called "kinetic energy." Kinetic energy is simply the motion of mass. So the more mass we can get moving in the proper sequence in the golf swing, the more kinetic energy or clubhead speed we can generate.

Another example of this type of physics law or formula would be the equation for the power of wind. That formula is V squared equals energy. For example, the V being velocity, if it were a five knot wind, the energy factor would be 25. If we substituted a 20 for the V and squared it, the energy factor would be 400. So with only a 15 knot increase in wind power, we've increased our energy factor approximately 20 times.

So what we're saying in simple terms is that the more velocity we can generate in body movement under control and the more mass we can put behind that movement, we will simply create a faster clubhead. The energy, in other words, translates into clubhead speed.

There are some other basic laws which will help us understand how we create torque, power, kinetic energy, and our goal, clubhead speed. Let's take a club and hold it straight above our head as shown in Photograph 6. If we now draw a line from our left shoulder to the tip of the club, it would measure somewhere between four and five feet long. Now, let's look at Photograph 7 and drop our line down to our left knee and measure from our left knee all the way up the left thigh, through the left shoulder, down through the left arm, up through the hand to the clubhead. This line would be between seven and eight feet long. This creates a longer spring in the body and creates a lower center of gravity for our power movement.

This would be like adding people onto an ice skating line. The more people we add, the faster the one at the end has to go. It's also like pulling back a bow string. The further back we pull it, the tighter it gets, the more torque we have in the body. It also might be like using a sling shot, pulling it all the way back till the rubber bands are stretched tight, so that the longer

Photograph 6.

the spring and the tighter we coil it, the more clubhead speed we will generate. Therefore, we are going to start our downswing with our knees to lower the center of gravity and to create the longest spring possible. Also, this gives us a bigger relationship in our swing arc to the size of the ball. So the bigger the swing arc, which is the circle or path the club travels in the backswing and downswing positions, we will be able to create a bigger ratio between ball and swing arc, and therefore generate clubhead speed.

There is another major law besides the energy formula that we need to know in order to effectively understand the physics laws in the swing, and the importance of the pieces and how they move. I call this the "inverted pyramid." Looking at Illustration 1 we see that we have a triangle standing on its tip. It is divided into three parts. The top part we will call the legs and the hips. The center part of the pyramid is the shoulders and arms and the tip

Photograph 7.

of the pyramid is the fast-polishing wrists. So what we are doing here is moving from large to intermediate to small. This creates torque in the body, like the old Indian burn when you took someone's wrist when you were a child and twisted it in counter-turning ways with your hands. Therefore, the legs and the hips are the major power sources of the golf swing. Now this does not relate to muscle strength. It related back earlier to the formula to mass and kinetic energy. So we don't have to be strong to hit a golf ball. We ust have to have mass in the proper sequence at the proper time under the proper position.

This is all overlaid by proper timing, which is the sequence of uncoiling, he tempo which is the metronome or the counting of the swing, and the hythm, which I call the dance step or the finesse of the swing. These will be covered in later chapters as we go over the nine parts of the swing. The

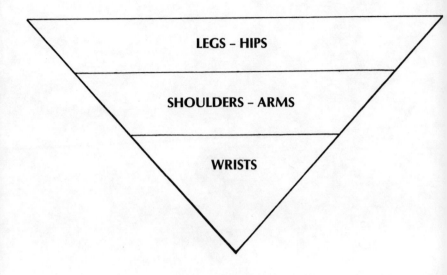

Illustration 1.

average golfer moves with his shoulders and arms first, his wrists second, and his legs and hips third. It's just like he snipped himself in half at the waist and swung with the upper body and had none of the mass moving to pull the clubhead down and into position.

These, then, are the three basic laws. The first, the energy formula for creating clubhead speed; the second, the relationship of ball size to swing arc; and the third, the inverted pyramid will give you a basic understanding of the secrets of the golf swing which are not understood by a great majority of golfers.

CHAPTER 6

THE DISEASES

There are eight major diseases or problems in golf. These relate to the swing, the club, and the clubhead and not to the problems that we encounter on the golf course itself. These eight categories do not exhaust the potential problems we have in the swing, but everything beyond these eight is a takeoff thereof, or a combination of these problems. In Illustration 2 I have shown these eight basic diseases.

We need, at this time, to define the target line so that we can decide what deviation we are making from it with the body movement or the clubhead. The target line is the direction in which we want the ball to fly. It might not necessarily be aiming at a green, it may be aiming at a point in the fairway from which we will be making another shot. The target line is the one down which we are trying to take our clubhead for as long and as straight as possible. It is a direct line from our left shoulder pointing left toward the desired target. If we laid a golf club on the ground and pointed it where we wanted the ball to go, this would be our target line.

Now we must have four things parallel or square to that target line: the feet, the knees, the hips and the shoulders. In other words, we are facing a brick wall squarely without turning any of those four parts to the right or to the left. With that target line in mind, any ball that curves drastically to the right with a clockwise spin, we call a "slice." It's counterpart is the "hook," where the ball curves drastically toward the left with a counterclockwise spin.

The "fade" is a ball that goes to the right of the target line, fairly straight to begin with, but tails or curls off at the end toward the right. This means that the clockwise spin of the ball was much less than in the slice, so as the ball begins to slow down, the dimples bite the air more and as it turns clockwise the ball tails to the right. In other words, the forward momentum is greater than the spin.

The "draw" is the same concept, only it tails off to the left. The counterclockwise spin is less just as in the fade. When we "push" a ball, it is as though we have turned our whole body on a lazy susan and hit the ball straight to the right of our intended target. The "pull" is a ball that is hit straight left of our intended target.

When we talk about hitting the ball "thin," we are hitting it below the equator or center, but not underneath the ball. It may be a quarter inch below center but it does not have the right trajectory. If we "top" a ball, we are hitting it above the equator and being a sphere as we talked about earlier, the ball will not get airborne and will dribble in front of us and stay

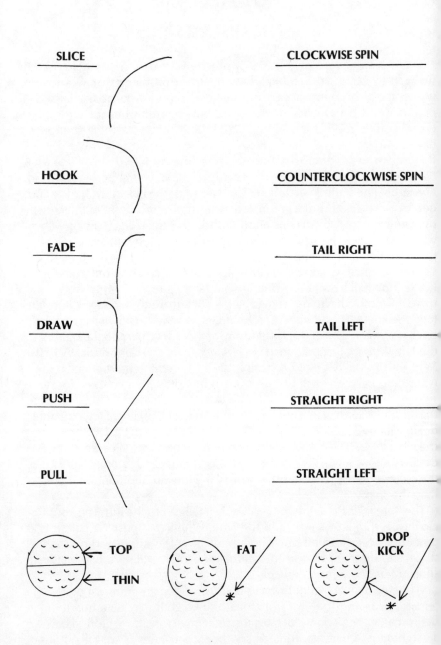

SLICE   CLOCKWISE SPIN

HOOK   COUNTERCLOCKWISE SPIN

FADE   TAIL RIGHT

DRAW   TAIL LEFT

PUSH   STRAIGHT RIGHT

PULL   STRAIGHT LEFT

TOP

THIN

FAT

DROP KICK

Illustration 2.

on the ground. A "fat" shot is one where we hit the ground behind the ball and either stop at that point with no contact or we "drop kick" which means we hit the ground and glance up and hit the ball, and in most cases in the upper half; such a ball will simply roll in front of us without getting airborne.

You will note that three of these problems go right of the target line and three go to the left of the target line. The other two have to do with where we contact the ball or not contacting it at all.

Most of the reasons why we do these eight things will be covered in later chapters as the particular cause and effect relationship comes out in that discussion. However, for a basic understanding I would like to take each of these items and give the basic reasons why they occur.

This chapter is by no means exhaustive on this subject, but in the book's entirety, the other reasons for the eight problems occurring will be brought out, but before doing this we need to know the difference between an opened or a closed club face.

If we were to stand with our toes on a target line, our left shoulder facing the target, and place our club so that the sole or bottom was also pointing straight down that line, we would have a square club face. This is shown in Photograph 8. If we rotate our arms and hands clockwise, the clubhead will turn to the right and the face will be pointing at a line to the right of our target line. This open club face position is shown in Photograph 9. If we turn our club face counterclockwise so that the face looks or points to the left of our target line, this is called a closed club face. This is shown in Photograph 10. Understanding this we will now proceed to a discussion of the two reasons why we slice a ball.

There are more reasons why we slice a ball, but as previously mentioned, these will come out as we develop the nine steps of our swing. Taking a club down the target line with the face open causes the ball to spin off the clubhead in a clockwise spin. As the dimples bite the air, this clockwise spin causes it to curve drastically to the right. The second major reason for a slice occurs when the clubhead travels a path from the outside to the inside or left of the target line. This occurs in either a square or open clubhead. The reasons these two things occur will be discussed later.

The hook is the opposite of a slice. Swinging the clubhead down the target line with the clubhead closed will cause a hook. Moving the clubhead down the target line from the inside to the outside of the target line either squared or closed will cause a hook. The most common cause of this problem is addressing the ball with a closed club face. In other words, the face aims left of the target line. Other causes, such as late hip turn or a flat-footed swing, can change our swing plane to more of a baseball swing or a horizontal plane which will make us swing around the hips and close the club face, hooking the ball left.

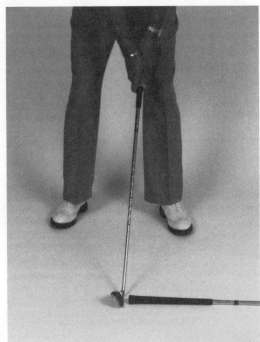

Photograph 8.

Photograph 9.

The push occurs when the clubhead is swung from inside to outside of the normal target line with the face open, then we create a new line straight to the right. This can be caused by hand position, lunging and shoulder plane. It is as if we were standing on a lazy susan and someone reached down and turned us slightly to the right and we would have a new straight line in that direction. The causes of these problems will be covered more as we develop the swing.

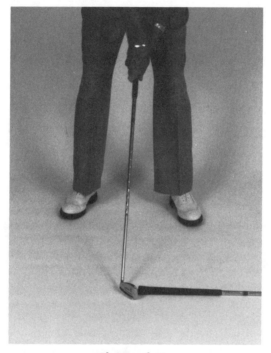

Photograph 10.

When we pull a ball the clubhead is traveling from the outside to the inside of our target line with a closed club face. A flat-footed swing or a high right shoulder also caused by looking up too early will flatten the swing plane and cause this condition. Chapter 10 will cover the cause and effect of this problem. The fade right and the draw left as shown in Illustration 2 are caused by the same problems as the slice and the hook, but by lesser degrees of error. The ball, therefore, has less side spin on it and the forward momentum makes the ball go straight and as it slows down, the side spin takes over and causes it to curve either right or left. Many advanced golfers use this technique of fading or drawing the ball to their advantage depending in some cases on how they want to come onto the green.

Topping occurs when striking a ball above the equator or above center. It is caused by our angle of attack, known as the swing arc, being in more of a V shape instead of round. Pushing too much with the right hand, or breaking the wrists into a concave position, allows the clubhead to lead the hands. These are two major reasons for topping. I call this swing a flat tire. There are other reasons that topping can occur. When the ball is too far forward in the stance, we will hit it on the upswing as the center of our downswing is equally between the feet. If the ball is too far forward, we bottom out the swing at center and catch it as we come up and top it. When we straighten the left leg on the downswing, stand up, raise the head too early, or fore-shorten the left arm, topping can result.

The thin shot, hitting below the center of the ball, is caused by the same problems as with the topped shot. Whereas the thin shot will get airborne to some degree, the topped shot will stay on the ground. When we hit a thin shot there are two strong areas that are suspect. One is straightening the left leg which occurs just before impact. The other is looking up or moving the head with the shoulder plane in the downswing. We only have three-fourths of an inch below the center of the ball in which to hit, so just a slight straightening either in the legs or raising the head causes us to hit the ball thin.

The fat shot comes in two forms. One is hitting the ball behind and missing it altogether or drop kicking by hitting the ground first and the ball second. The first action, even though we don't hit the ball, is counted as a stroke. Fat shots are caused by lack of weight shift to the left in our downswing. Too much strength in the right hand which causes pushing or shoving of the club in a downward path, fly-casting with the wrists from the top of our swing, reversing our weight back on our right foot, and bad timing in our four-step sequence to the downswing, as covered in the downswing chapter, are also possible causes of the fat shot.

CHAPTER 7

THE GRIP

In the chapters that follow we are going to cover the nine parts of the swing. Each part is like a piece of the puzzle and when we put it together we will have a total picture which is our golf swing. We will divide the nine parts of the golf swing into what we call fixed or non-moving positions and moving positions. The grip is one of the fixed positions, which means we can take our time because the ball will remain in place until we get into our moving positions, so there's no hurry in setting our grip. We can take our time in getting our hands set.

Now the backswing must be developed first and it has two reasons for existing. One is to get good position preparing to strike the ball. The other we call torque, or the winding up of the spring in the body.

We are now going to start the process of isolating the muscle areas toward building muscle memories. We will start with the left hand, which we will call the lead hand as it faces or is closer to the target. Now a word to left-handers playing with a left-handed stance. Simply reverse everything I'm saying and this will then translate into the correct applications for you as a left-hander.

In starting out to set the left hand on the grip of the club, we are going to start with our first exercise. This is shown in Photograph 11. We hold the club between the thumb and forefinger of the left hand and pinch together at the base of the two fingers. This will give you the correct feel of the action that we use when we press the finger together to form a straight line. Now turn the palm up and we will look at two points across which we will lay the club. The first joint of the left forefinger and a line below the little finger. These are shown in Photograph 12. The club is laid across these two points and the hand rolled over until two knuckles, the first being the index finger and the second the middle finger, are visible. The line formed by the thumb and forefinger points to the right eye. See Photograph 13. The buildup of a pad in the left hand and three fingers starting with the little finger holding the club create a vice-like action we are looking for. This pad ends at the cap of the club and is in the same place for all clubs in full swing. This is shown in Photograph 14.

The right hand is going to be placed on the club in such a way as to make it passive. There are three ways that we're going to make the right hand submissive to the left hand. Hold the right hand in front of you, pinching the thumb and forefinger together, forming a line which stops at the bottom knuckle of the thumb of the right hand. You'll see this in Photograph 15. Keeping the thumb and forefinger pinched together, turn the palm upward. You will notice in Photograph 16 that we have a groove or valley formed between the two pads of the right hand.

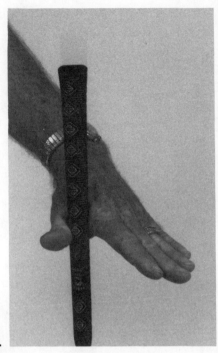

Photograph 11.

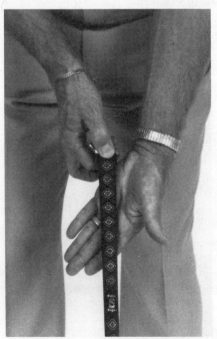

Photograph 12.

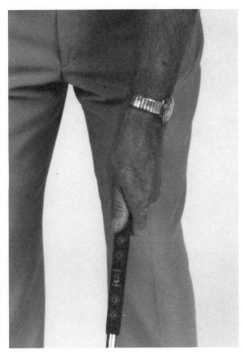

Photograph 13.

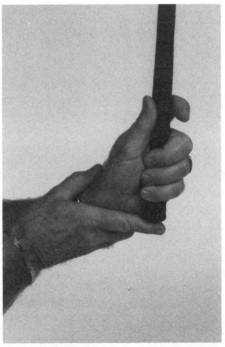

Photograph 14.

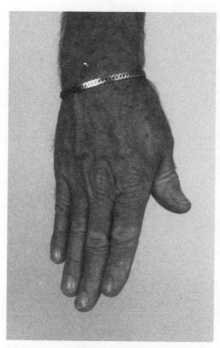

Photograph 15.

We're going to place this valley over the knuckle in the left hand. The little finger of the right hand will now rest on top of the forefinger of the left hand. The next two fingers slide down until they touch the forefinger of the left hand. This is shown in Photograph 17. The thumb and the forefinger, which have been pinched together to form a straight line, are placed on the club fairly loosely so that the line goes to the right eye and the two knuckles on the right hand are visible as we look down at the hands. Both hands together must now be in a position where both lines formed by each of the thumbs and forefingers point to the right eye. With pressure being applied on the last three fingers of the left hand and the middle two fingers of the right hand, we have really five fingers that are gripping, three on the left and two on the right, and five fingers that are passive. See Photograph 18. The hands are facing each other in a palm-to-palm type of position. The hands, as they get used to the grip, will work together as a unit. When we bring the club up to a perpendicular position at arms length in front of us, we can see the lines to the right eye and the two knuckles visible. These are the major checkpoints in the hands. See Photograph 19.

As we started this chapter, I mentioned three ways we can make the right side passive. The first is the line to the right eye which puts the hand in an

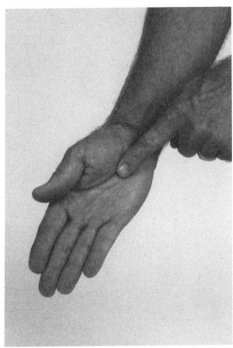

Photograph 16.

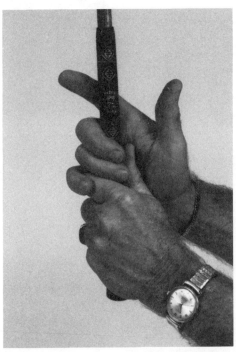

Photograph 17.

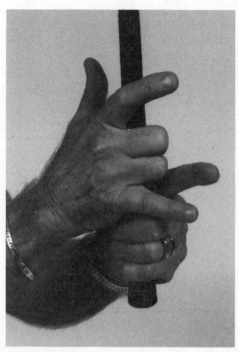

Photograph 18.

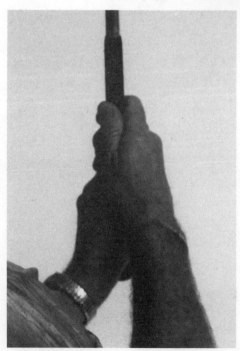

Photograph 19.

abnormal position. If we were going to use a hammer with our right hand, this line would point out over our right shoulder. So by turning the palm to the target, we have put the right hand in a soft position. By holding the club with only two fingers of the right hand, we will take away strength, which would be compounded by adding the other three fingers. The third way to make the right hand passive is simply to relax the hand and the arm so that we don't see any white knuckles and we feel a very soft grip on the club.

Our next exercise is shown in Photograph 20 where we hold the club in the right hand, gripping the fingers at the bottom of the grip, practicing letting the club slide down toward the end, and then stopping the sliding motion. This exercise serves two purposes: to give us the feel of the two fingers doing the gripping, and to feel the amount of pressure used in guiding the club with the right hand.

Photograph 20.

CHAPTER 8

STANCE, POSTURE AND ALIGNMENT

The stance is another one of our fixed positions. It refers to the feet only. We place our heels approximately shoulder width apart with our toes straight ahead facing the target line as though we were standing in a box. This is called a square stance. Now turn the left foot out between 30 and 45 degrees. this action will take the twisting motion off the ankle when we make our downswing later on. The right foot remains straight, the left foot turned out slightly. This position is shown in Photograph 21. The weight should be equally distributed on both feet. However, we want the weight to

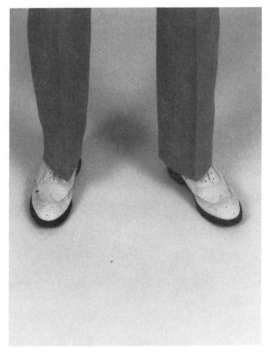

Photograph 21.

be on the inside of the feet and toward the heels. This is accomplished by pressing the knees in slightly toward center. This is a slightly knock-kneed position. We should now be able to pat our toes by raising them up and down as the weight lies toward the heels. This will keep our center of gravity through the body as we make our swing and keep the centrifugal force of the downswing from allowing us to fall forward.

In Photograph 22, the club lying against our toes is the target line. At this point, it is important to understand what we mean by an open or a closed stance. If we turn our back totally to the target, we are completely closed. As we turn our feet back to line up with the toes touching the club, at any point between back to target and in between, is closed. When our toes touch our club again, we are now square. As we continue to turn until we face the target squarely with our shoulders, we are now open in our stance. At any point along the path that we take from square to facing the target is the open stance. So then, when we are slightly closed in our stance, our target line points to the right and if we are slightly opened, the target line points to the left. When we point our target line to the right, we generally swing outside and hook the ball, and when we turn our target line to the left, we swing inside and slice the ball. Our goal, then, is to keep our club down the target line for as long and as straight as possible.

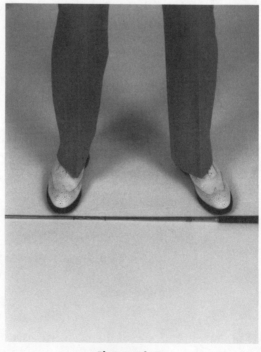

Photograph 22.

The posture in the golf address position refers to knee bends and back bends. We will start first with the knee bends. This will lead us to a series of three exercises shown in Photographs 23, 24 and 25. First we hold the clubhead as though it were a pistol grip and place the cap of the club on the floor approximately four to six inches straight out from or opposite our left ankle. The club should be perpendicular and not pushed forward or backward. The goal in this exercise is to see how much knee bend is necessary in the stance position.

The stance position is also one of our fixed or non-moving positions. The goal is to try to get enough knee bend to be able to slide the knees laterally left to touch the club but with no more than is necessary to accomplish this movement. Let's start off stiff-legged and try to move our knees left. You will notice that this is impossible because our joints don't move that way. If I add a little bend, I can move slightly left; if I add a little more, I can touch the club as shown in Photograph 23.

The next exercise does the same thing, but just shows us another way so

Photograph 23.

Photograph 24.

that we can reinforce what we are trying to do. In Photograph 24 we hold the club straight down in the right hand at the hosel. We place the club against our thighs, touching both and pointing it to the target. We now slide the knees left and hold the club steady so that we slide along the club without our left knee pulling away, leaving a gap between the club and our left thigh. This exercise keeps us moving straight down the target line.

Next, as shown in Photograph 25, we are going to pinch the club between the thumb and forefinger of each hand and hold it against the thighs as though the pinching points were bolts that were set into our legs, so that when we move left, we move the legs together. The purpose of this exercise is to show that we don't move one leg or the other independently, but as a unit. If you feel your pinched fingers against the thighs sliding, then you know that the leg is pulling away from the other.

By practicing these three exercises you will quickly learn how much knee bend we have in the lower body. Also remember from our discussion on the stance that the knees are in slightly with the weight inside of the feet and toward the heels.

The next bend we have in the posture position is the back bend. This is an area that is not understood clearly by most golfers. So we are going to do

Photograph 25.

another exercise as shown in Photograph 26. We place the club behind our back, stand up straight, stomach in, chest out, and touch the club with the back of our head. We now bow forward from the waist and let our left arm hand down naturally over the left thigh. We bend enough at the waist to allow the left hand to move out approximately five to six inches from the left thigh. At this point we have enough back bend to be able to swing our hands through the shot and clear our hips and have the correct shoulder plane, which will be discussed later. If we continue to bow forward, our hands will go further out from the body and serve no useful purpose, so the degree of back bend determines hand position.

The head is dropped down just enough to see the ball, but no further. If we bury the chin into the chest, our head will be pushed out of the way prematurely in the downswing moves. When we place the club in the hands at this point, and assuming that the ball is centered, you will notice that our hands are forward or in front of the ball approximately six inches.

We have another checkpoint to determine if the hands are set properly and the degree of back bend is adequate. We call this checkpoint a plumb line. In Photograph 27, you will notice that the club is hanging straight down from the right eye. The club should fall across a point where the grip meets

Photograph 26.

Photograph 27.

the steel shaft. If the plumb line crosses our hands, we are either too upright, or the hands are too far out from the body. If the plumb line bisects the steel shaft, we're either bent over too far or our hands are pulled in too close to the body. This is a very good checkpoint to show proper distance of the left hand from the body and the proper degree of back bend.

In practicing the back bend exercise shown in Photograph 26, you will notice that we do not round our back over the ball, but we bow from the waist to maintain a straight back. This is very important as we develop our backswing shoulder turns.

In the alignment phase of our posture and stance positions, we should imagine that we are facing a brick wall. the feet, knees, hips and shoulders must all be parallel to that brick wall. It's possible for us to have our feet squared to the wall and our shoulders and hips open. If we feel that we have a pin through our hip and bow forward squarely instead of twisting slightly to the left, we will feel this alignment, or that we are facing the brick wall.

With the proper grip, stance, posture and alignment, we are now in the position of address. This is the position we take in preparing to make our first move, which is called the "takeaway." When we're in the position of address, we try to keep the left side, the arm and the hand, and the grip firm, and the right side relaxed which will help lead us to left side control. We have already talked about ways to make the right hand passive in the last chapter.

CHAPTER 9

TAKEAWAY AND BACKSWING

We have now completed our fixed or non-moving positions. The next four chapters will discuss the moving sequences used during the full swing. Remember that the ball is still stationary. There is no hurry in making our first move called the takeaway.

From the position of address, place the ball in the middle of our stance, or equally between the feet. The hands are on the inside of the left leg with the clubhead square to the target line. With the left arm dominating, take the clubhead straight back along the target line to the right foot without turning the hips. Still not turning the hips, draw the clubhead slightly inside the target line to hip high, forming a 45 degree clubhead angle, keeping the left wrist and left forearm in a straight line.

That this point, waist high of the takeaway, we have two checkpoints. These checkpoints are shown in Photograph 28. The cap of the club, or the shaft, points straight to the target. The clubhead, as we turn our head right and look at it, has a sole line, or the bottom of the club is at a 45 degree angle. There's no leg movement, no head movement, no wrist movement at this point as the club is drawn back by the left shoulder and from the left shoulder to the clubhead we have one long straight welded pipe. There's no pronation of the wrists at this point into the takeaway. This position is also called a "quarter swing." This swing is also used near the green, specifically in the low pitch or pitch and run shot.

All the way through the takeaway and backswing, in addition to keeping our head still, we need to keep our eye on the ball. I prefer to be more specific and tell my students to pick a dimple on the top of the ball and focus in on that particular dimple. This narrows down the area that we're looking at and forces us to be specific. You might also pretend you were a person standing beside yourself watching yourself hit the ball. These two tips will help you a great deal in keeping your head steady through the backswing, downswing and impact. I consider the takeaway completed when the club is in its waist-high position and we are maintaining our two checkpoints.

The next three steps we will call the backswing. The wrist-cocking action comes next and is actually a vertical movement of the wrist to take the left thumb to what I call the thumbs up position. At this point the club is now vertical or pointing straight to the ground. The wrist does not move in a horizontal fashion, either concave or convex. The wrist-cocking action is limited by the amount of the vertical wrist motion we can physically handle. In Photograph 29A we have the first stage of an exercise where we reach

Photograph 28.

Photograph 29A.

down and pull our left thumb straight up as far as it will go. This exercise is done without a club.

In Photograph 29B, we take our right hand and place it underneath our left and turn until our thumb points up. This is the position I was describing earlier. If we added a club to our hands, we would now have a right angle formed by our left arm and the club shaft. This position is also called the "half-swing." The half-swing is used in our sand traps or bunkers and in a high pitch shot. So all of these positions through which we pass in a backswing are used at different times while we are playing golf.

Photograph 29B.

After the wrists have cocked to the thumbs up position, our third move in the timing sequence of the backswing is the right shoulder turning up, or if you wish, the left shoulder continues to turn under the chin. At this point our back is to the target and our hips are forced to turn to a 45 degree angle. The weight still remains inside and to the rear on both feet. The left knee turns in against the right braced leg. The heels stay on the ground and we roll in slightly on the inside of the left foot. I do not believe in lifting the left heel. In checking out a long list of professionals you will find some that do and some that don't. But in the more modern golf swing, with the younger golfers coming along, the left heel is kept firmly on the ground.

Photograph 30.

In Photograph 30 you will notice I have placed my club along the right leg and this is what we call the brace or the fence post against which we move. In Photograph 31 you will notice the 45 degree hip turn that I talked about as the fourth step in the backswing. It is most important that we think as if we were standing in a barrel and turning within the barrel, but not touching the sides. There is no lateral weight shift in either direction, nor is there an overturning of the hips which would help create a flat swing. The club is now up over the right shoulder and this is the plane that we are looking for in the backswing. If we drop the club down touching the shoulder as shown in Photograph 32, we would have the proper position for the hands, so the club goes from the right shoulder in the backswing to the left shoulder in the finish.

Photograph 31.

Photograph 32.

Throughout these four steps of the backswing, the left arm remains as straight as possible. However, it does not have to be locked at the elbow. The right elbow remains in as close to the right hip as possible, pointing toward the ground. It also forms the letter "L" as we move into the backswing. At this point we want to be careful not to fly or raise the right elbow to a horizontal position.

What we have covered are the four steps to the backswing. These steps are called "timing." Timing is a movement of parts in a sequence, an orderly sequence so that we have now moved our left shoulder, wrists, right shoulder and hips.

There are several problems that the average golfer runs into in taking the backswing position. One is standing up with the legs, so we must maintain the bends in the knees and the bend in the back. Placing too much weight outside of the right foot puts us into a timing problem in the downswing where we're trying to play catch-up as we attempt to get back at the ball in the proper downswing timing sequences which will be discussed in the next chapter. I call this "reaching up to touch bottom." Breaking the left arm drastically so that the club drops almost on our shoulder creates fly-casting in our downswing and takes tension off the rubber band or spring that we're winding up in the backswing. Breaking or cupping the left wrist as we go into the backswing is a major problem for some golfers. That's why I placed Photographs 29A and 29B into the text, which is a very fine exercise to help you feel the right kind of wrist-cocking motion. Bringing the head straight up, and simply allowing your eyes to come off the dimple on the ball is another problem because watching the dimple on the ball throughout the backswing takes a fair amount of concentration. So the key to the takeaway and backswing moves again are left shoulder, wrists, right shoulder up and hips forced.

The other major problem a lot of golfers have is a hip turn which starts early and is not forced as the shoulders turn. Picking up the club early is another major fault in this area. If we take it back long and low with the left shoulder past the right foot and then move into our wrist-cocking and shoulder turns we will eiminate what I call the V plane and make our swing arc round.

The full swing never dips the club beyond parallel to the ground at the top of the backswing. The three-quarter swing would be between that point and 45 degrees from the half-swing or the thumbs up position. For older people this is a good swing to work towards and can be used to play a very successful and low scoring golf game. The difference between the three-quarter swing as shown in Photograph 33 and the full swing is small enough that we will not sacrifice a great deal of distance.

Remembering that the game is made up of a number of areas, (i.e. full swing, close game, putting, special conditions of the golf course, special conditions caused by nature), we can see that all of these things combine to make a complete score during a round of golf so we don't need to rely on a few extra yards on a drive if we are not able to make that particular move. I feel that too much emphasis has been placed on the full swing where the club is parallel at the top, and also with the influence of television we see this swing a lot with the younger fellows on the tour. But now that the senior tour is coming strongly into its own, we will see more of the three-quarter

Photograph 33.

swings and still some very fine scores by the seniors in their tournaments. I'm mentioning this because we have a population age shift taking place where many older people are playing recreational golf in a lot of the retirement communities. It is not necessary to think that we're a kid again and worry about a full swing. A well positioned three-quarter swing which will deliver the clubhead down the target line for as long and as straight as possible with a reasonable amount of speed in proper timing will give good direction and distance.

CHAPTER 10

DOWNSWING

The downswing movements, timing sequences, and tempo are the three most misunderstood areas in the golf swing. They're also the most difficult to master. Because they're difficult we will approach them from several different angles in order to make sure we completely comprehend what we're trying to do.

Learning starts with understanding. In the golf swing we must move from thinking to doing or from the brain to body reflex. We must now shift gears from the upper body backswing moves to the lower body downswing moves. The downswing timing sequence which uncoils the spring created by the backswing is as follows: knees, right hip, left shoulder and wrists. This is very important. If you refer back to Chapter 5, entitled "The Physics Laws," it will help you understand the movement of mass from the large leg and hip areas through the intermediate shoulders and arms to the fast-polishing wrist.

We will start the knees moving by reviewing three lateral shifting exercises shown in Photographs 23, 24 and 25. These three exercises demonstrate the first movement in the downswing. If the knees move first, they pull the hands down as shown in Photography 34. The second timing movement in the downswing is a turning of the right hip, 45 degrees toward the target. This position, as shown in Photograph 35, will remain throughout impact and the two extension moves shown later. This move pulls the hands further in position toward impact.

As yet, we have not used the upper body. There's no hand movement, no arm movement, no shoulder movement. These three areas move, but only as pulled by the weight shift and hip turn. Our weight is now 70 percent left and 30 percent right. We are balanced on the big toe of the right foot. The legs remain flexed.

In other to further understand the first two movements of the downswing, we will introduce the first of three downswing formulas. Number one is called the "slide-touch-turn." We place the club four to six inches off the left ankle and perpendicular to the ground. The right hand is on the hip. Make the lateral knee move. When the club is touched, push the right hip through until it faces the target as shown in Photograph 36.

We have three checkpoints which will help to assure correct position: (1) The right knee is toward the target or pointing at the target, (2) The right toe points to the ground, and (3) The left leg remains flexed.

Do not push off the right foot as though you were a runner pushing off a starting block. This move is a weight shift left and a hip turn, which creates a

Photograph 34.

Photograph 35.

thigh position as shown in Photograph 37. Notice that the right leg is not straight.

The third moving part of the downswing is the pulling left shoulder. These three moves happen very quickly, and so close together, we cannot see where one begins and the other leaves off. This smooth uncoiling of the lateral shift, right hip turn, and left arm pulling is called "rhythm."

Photograph 36.

The second downswing formula is called the "shift-pivot-pull." We hold the club in our left hand, right hand behind the back. We take about a half backswing shown in Photograph 38. We then shift laterally left with the knees, turn the right hip, and then pull the club with the left shoulder to the position of finish, shown in Photograph 39. At this point, we should be able to reach up and connect our right hand in grip position without any moves in the rest of our body. In other words, the position in which we finish the exercise is the same position in which we finish our short irons and mid-irons, except our right hand is on the club.

The fourth moving part of the downswing timing sequence is the uncocking of the wrists. This happens naturally in most cases without a conscious

Photograph 37.

Photograph 38.

Photograph 39.

effort. Before the release of the wrists, the letter "L" is formed by the club shaft and left arm as shown in Photograph 40.

Photograph 40.

The final formula for timing the downswing is called the "rule-of-opposites." This rule means that the left shoulder and the right hip work together. These are opposite quarters of our body. If we pull with the left shoulder and push the right hip through at the same time, we will be reasonably well-timed.

In all of these movements and formulas, the head remains still and the eye on a dimple of an imaginary ball. So remember the three formulas that will aid you in the difficult downswing sequence: the "slide-touch-turn," the "shift-pivot-pull," and the "rule-of-opposites."

In addition to the three formulas, we have two downswing exercises that will give us correct position and timing. The first is the arm swing exercise.

We hook the head of the club in the crook of the left elbow and take our normal address position, with the club touching our right shoulder. We have the knees bent, back bent, and right hand over the left thigh. This is shown in Photograph 41A. Take a one-half backswing to thumb up. We shift left with the knees six to eight inches, turn the right hip 45 degrees, and the V formed by the grip and the right wrist should be behind the hips as shown in Photograph 41B. Let the right arm swing freely behind the hip (see Photograph 41C). If we can accomplish this move, it means that our legs and hips are leading the swing and the arms and wrists are being held back.

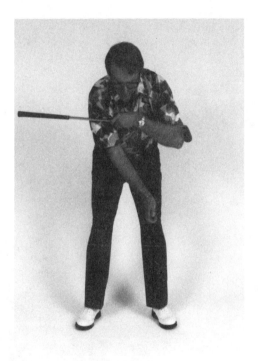

Photograph 41A.

The second exercise is called the club swinging exercise. The club is pinched between the thumb and forefinger of the left hand. The last three fingers are closed. The club is held at arms length in line with the left shoulder, so that the left arm and shoulder plane form a right angle. This is shown in Photograph 42A. The right hand is held palm up to support the club. The club is parallel to the ground and shoulder high. The club is released by the right hand and swings into the position shown in Photo-

Photograph 41B.

Photograph 41C.

Photograph 42A.

graph 42B. When the club swings back to its original position, we put the right hand under the club palm down this time, but not allowing the hand to touch the shaft. This is shown in Photograph 42C. As the club starts down in a natural pendulum swing, we shift and pivot, but move the right hand and left shoulder in the rhythm dictated by the natural swinging club. Do not let the club bump into the right hand. In other words, we must swing fast enough to get out of the way of the swinging club. The finished position is shown in Photograph 42D, with the left hand holding the club and the three lower body checkpoints in effect.

The downswing timing sequence, then, is knees, right hip, left shoulder and wrists. This uncoils the body flowing from our lowest center of gravity that we're able to move, the knees, and flows up through the hips, left shoulder, down through the left arm and to the wrists. This four-sequence move is timed by the exercises and formulas given earlier in the chapter.

Photograph 42B.

Photograph 42C.

Photograph 42D.

CHAPTER 11

IMPACT

Photograph 43.

The impact position is shown in Photograph 43. We can actually practice this position as a stop-action exercise. We do this by taking a normal address position. Let's use a 5-iron for this particular exercise. Shift the legs left into the normal downswing position. Turn the right hip 45 degrees, balance on the big toe of the right foot. The weight should be distributed approximately 70 percent on the left foot and 30 percent on the inside of the right foot. Make sure the hands stay in line with the left thigh, not center. The club is still grounded at the center position. The head has not moved and we are still looking at the dimple on the ball. The left arm must be fully extended on impact with the full extention maintained until hip high of the follow-through. The back of the left wrist and forearm must be at a straight line relationship so that the club face is square to the target at impact.

In the last chapter we talked about the four timing sequences in the downswing. There is another factor we must consider as we move through the takeaway to impact progressions. It is called "tempo." Tempo is like a metronome whereas timing is like a pendulum. A metronome is a device for marking time. In the case of the golf swing, we count one, two, pause, three, or one, two, pause, shift. The counts one and two take us from address to the top of the backswing. The pause at the top is like shifting gears in a car. It allows the upper body moves of the backswing to shift into the lower body moves of the downswing. The count of three is the downswing to impact. In other words, we wind up the backswing much slower than we move the downswing. It is a common fault for golfers to take the club back much too quickly as if the ball were going to jump away from them like a frog. Remember, we are hitting a stationary target.

The woods start down slower and gain momentum from shoulder high to impact. Think of the woods as a truck moving downhill slowly. At the bottom of the hill, the wood or truck is moving very fast, say moving over 100 miles per hour. The irons are like a sports car. They move faster from the top and gain speed earlier. In either case, we must pull with the left arm and keep the right hand passive. At impact, the back of the left hand faces toward the target. This position is shown in Photograph 44. The tendency in the downswing is to push or shove the club instead of pulling it. We cannot stop the club at impact when actually swinging at a ball, but by using this stop-action exercise, shown in Photograph 43, we can continue building our reflexes and muscle memories by doing and not just thinking.

Photograph 44.

CHAPTER 12

FOLLOW-THROUGH AND BALANCE

There are two major positions of importance in the follow-through. They are called low extension and high extension. As each has an individual function, we will take them one at a time.

Photograph 45A.

The low extension position is shown in Photographs 45A and 45B. Our hips are still turned 45 degrees in the same position that they were at impact. The low extension position is the only place in the total swing arc where the arms are both straight. The club cap or grip points into the stomach. We have a position that looks like the letter "Y" formed by the arms and the club. We can see this in Photograph 45A. The clubhead is in a position of 45 degrees as it is turned over slightly through the supination of the hands as we pass through impact. The shoulder plane is still down 45 degrees and our

Photograph 45B.

head has not moved. Our head has stayed in place or still from the address position through takeaway, backswing, downswing, impact and low extension. The right hand is on top of the club caused by the supination of the left hand.

The high extension position is shown in Photograph 46. At this point the shoulder and chin are touching. The high extension position is also called the "break point." At the break point the arms bend to form the letter "L" and the grip points to target. In the high extension the hips are still at the 45 degree turn position. The shoulder plane is still at the 45 degree down position. The legs have remained flexed throughout the entire swing as straightening would pull us off the ball and either cause topping or a thin shot.

As we move into the five checkpoint finish, shown in Photograph 47, the shoulder pushes the head up into position. We do not have to think consciously about moving the chin in the golf swing. If we keep the head still, the shoulder plane, as it moves through the low and high extensions, will push the head up without a conscious effort on our part. There is a straight line relationship between the arm and the club in the high extension position. In other words, we can draw a line from the shoulder through the

Photograph 46.

Photograph 47.

hands to the clubhead and straight out to the target. The toe of our club becomes our gunsight that points where we want the ball to go.

In the five checkpoint finish, we have four things pointing to the target: grip, right elbow, right knee and hips. The toe points to the ground. I call this the statue position where we pose at the end of the swing. The weight must be distributed 95 percent on the outside of the left foot and 5 percent on the toe of the right foot. The only way we can maintain our balance is to move into a C-shape arch. This keeps our center of gravity over the ball.

One of the best exercises you can do to help this position is shown in Photograph 48. We place the club against our shoulders and turn to the five checkpoint finish with the shoulder plane parallel to the ground. We push back on the club until our head is over the center of our stance or where the ball used to be. After pushing back to the C-shape arch, turn the shoulder plane down to point the club toward the ground at a 45 degree angle.

Photograph 48.

Another exercise that will help you to extend through the two positions just covered is shown in Photograph 49A. We hook the club in the crook of the right elbow and grasp it on the steel shaft with the right hand. We then take a half-backswing called "thumbs up" (shown in Photograph 49B). Next make the knee shift and right hip turn. Extend the arm and club straight out pointing it to the target. This is shown in Photograph 49C. This exercise is designed to give us direction to the target as most people at this time tend to swing inside or to the left due to late timing or raised right shoulder.

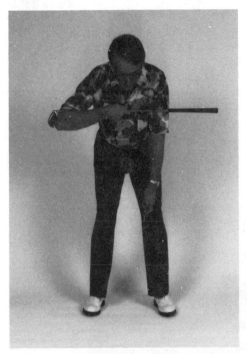

Photograph 49A.

Photographs 50A and 50B show the two finished positions that we use in the five checkpoints. Looking just at the grip in Photograph 50A, you will note that it points to the target. We point the grip in this position when we use the 5 through 9-irons and full wedge. Photograph 50B shows the finish for the long irons, Nos. 2, 3, 4 and the woods. In this finish the grip points 45 degrees to the left of the target line. The reason for this finish is the need for a breaking action. The long irons and the woods having longer shafts, and in the case of the woods, more mass at the heads, requires a longer time to stop

Photograph 49B.

Photograph 49C.

Photograph 50A.

Photograph 50B.

the club. If we stop the long irons and woods in position shown in Photograph 50A, we would be slowing down prior to impact. When we move into this long iron and wood position, the elbows are still about eight to 10 inches apart forming the letter "L." The movement happens because we twist more at the waist. The waist then becomes our brake. Notice in the five checkpoint finish position that our shoulder and chin are still touching, but our head is pushed into a position where we can glance out and follow the path of the ball. Never look between the arms.

Photograph 51A.

In Photograph 51A we are showing an exercise called the "box" exercise. You take two clubs, placing one parallel to your foot line at address, and the other at a right angle to it. When we address the ball, we are squared to the first club. When we are at the impact position, we are facing 45 degrees or toward the corner of the box (see Photograph 51B). When we finish we are facing the left club (see Photograph 51C). This tells us then that we only move 90 degrees in our total swing as we go from address to finish.

Photograph 51B.

Photograph 51C.

There are several faults that can occur in the positions of low extension, high extension and finish. The first of these is blocking, where the right hand has too much control and turns the club open as we see in Photograph 52. The ball will go to the right in either a slice, push or fade. A correction for this particular move is to supinate or turn over the hands as they pass through impact. This move must be made early to allow enough time for the brain to send a message to the body. We start thinking about turning the hands over at waist high of the downswing. If the ball still goes off to the right, we think higher, more up toward the right shoulder. Somewhere between the right shoulder and waist high we will be able to turn the hands over and make the ball go straight. If you have very sharp reflexes, you may make the ball hook by doing this exercise. If the ball hooks, simply think of turning the hands over a little bit later in the downswing. It is very important to think of the left hand doing the turning only. If we think of both hands, our right hand will probably do what it did to cause the original fault.

Photograph 52.

Photograph 53.

Another problem in low extension is what we call "pulling the plug." What we are doing is bending our arms to shorten the distance between clubhead and shoulders. This is shown in Photograph 53. The way to correct this fault is to place the ball in a tee, take a 5-iron and swing to a half-backswing position, which points the club perpendicular to the ground, and stop at the low extension position thinking of hitting through the ball and not at the ball. You must put on the brakes as though the clubhead were bumping into a wall in front of you. If you practice this for a period of time, you will be able to stop the swing with the arms straight out and eliminate elbow bending.

The next fault we call "lunging," or "bending at the waist" so that our head is in front of our left foot. The C-shape arching exercise will help correct this. The problem is shown in Photograph 54.

A very common fault is remaining flat-footed which causes a baseball type swing. Without the hips being cleared, we swing around ourself and the club points to the left and we are bent at the waist. This is shown in Photograph 55.

Collapsing the elbows or laying the club on the shoulder is shown in Photograph 56. The hands should be high in the finish position but the arms

Photograph 54.

are not straight. Refer back to the five checkpoint finish and you will notice the letter "L" position.

To sum up this chapter, the low extension position has the arms straight, club pointing to stomach, letter Y, and club to target. The head is still down.

The high extension causes the head to be forced up and the arms to break into our final finish position.

The five checkpoints show us that we are correct throughout the body. The C-shape arch keeps our center of gravity over the ball.

Photograph 55.

Photograph 56.

CHAPTER 13

LOW PITCH

The low pitch shot is also called the pitch and run. The pitching iron is the most commonly used club, however, a sand wedge is a good substitute if a higher trajectory or less run is needed.

We use this shot five yards to 25 yards from our landing spot on the green. As it is a running shot, we will need to divide the distance from the edge of the green to the hole into sections. If the grass is level, we try to land the ball half way between the edge and the cup. If the green is uphill, land two-thirds of the distance from the edge of the green to the cup. If the green is downhill, land one-third into the green or two-thirds from the flag stick. If we have a steep downhill grade, we need to bump the ball. A bump shot is one which hits just before the green and skips onto the green, rolling up to the cup. This is like skipping a pebble across the water. When we bump the longer grass before the green, it slows the ball down as it hops onto the green.

In the address position our feet are eight to 10 inches apart. The stance is open. This means our foot line points to the left of the target, however, our shoulder line points to the target. The ball is placed in the center of the stance. This is the only shot in which we pre-shift our weight to the left. This is shown in Photograph 57. This photograph also shows the backswing leg position. The weight is as far left as it would be if we shifted into a full downswing position. In other words, we cannot go any further left with our knees. The knees are locked in place and the legs remain flexed. As a rule of thumb, when we pre-shift, the legs will not be used in the swing. The back bend is normal. This is also the only swing where we set our hands last. I place the club close to the ball with the face aiming down the target line. Then slide the left hand down the grip until the left arm is straight. You will end up choked down two to three inches. The hands are forward over the left thigh about three inches out. This is half as far out as in the full swing.

In the backswing we use an early wrist-cocking action and a little shoulder turn. The club is never taken back further than parallel to the ground. This position is about waist high. We hit down and through by pulling with the left shoulder and releasing the wrists. We stop the club at knee high of the follow-through. This would be similar to the low extension position in the full swing. There is no re-cocking of the wrists. The sole line of the club is turned 45 degrees when the shot is complete. The toe of the club points toward the target (see Photograph 57A). The left arm is straight. The grip points up the right arm.

Photograph 57.

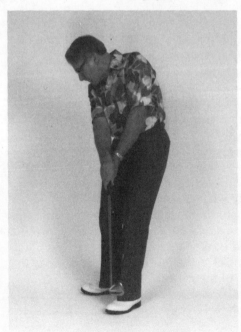

Photograph 57A.

The most important point to remember in this part of the swing concerns the tempo. The mechanical part of the swing, waist high backswing to knee high finish, is always the same. The tempo or speed is varied depending on how far we want the ball to go. Our thought process is slow and quick. We must slow down the backswing and accelerate the downswing. By doing this slow and quick tempo, we will not hit fat, or dribble the ball a few feet in front of us. The ball action has a nice soft jump to the green, then a roll to the cup. This shot covers a lot of territory around the green so the pitching iron is very important in your arsenal of weapons.

CHAPTER 14

HIGH PITCH

We use the high pitch shot to cover an area 25 to 60 yards from the hole. It is a high-flying shot which tends to stop quickly. Therefore, we do not pick landing spots on the green as we did in the low pitch, except to aim directly at the flag. You will note that the high pitch shot takes over where the low pitch leaves off.

We use either the pitching wedge or sand iron to execute this shot. The sand iron will fly the ball higher and shorten the distance. It is a good choice for getting over a tree close to the green. It is also a good choice for a downhill green.

The stance is narrow and square. The feet are about 15 inches apart. The weight is equally distributed inside and toward the heels like the full swing stance. The ball is played center. The swing being one-half-to-one-half means the club is taken back to the thumbs up or perpendicular backswing position. This is shown in Photograph 58.

The backswing timing sequence is left shoulder, wrists, and slight hip turn. The downswing timing is shift, right hip turn, pull and wrists. We stop at the one-half finish as shown in Photograph 59. The club shaft in the finish position is now our gunsight directly to the target. If we sight across the shaft in the half-swing finish, we should see the ball in that line. The swing is mechanical. The tempo is one, two, pause, three, just like the full swing. In fact, this shot is a miniature full swing. The hips finish 45 degrees through in the same position as high extension used in the full swing.

The high pitch shot has a lot of finesse using soft hands. Even though it is a mechanical swing, it is a flowing move in the rhythm. It is one of the more difficult shots to play because the downswing timing sequence must be exact. If you do not shift the knees early, followed by a one-half right hip turn, it is easy to hit this shot fat. Your head must remain still throughout the entire swing. It does not move until after the finish is held for two or three seconds.

If you get used to posing like a statue, the swing arc will remain round resulting in a high lofted shot, which lands softly on the green with little or no roll.

There is a variation of the high pitch shot called the "cut" shot. Everything remains the same except the clubhead is laid open, not a little opened, but drastically open. The result is a very high shot with great stopping power. This cut shot can be used within the low pitch range up to 25 yards, where you might be going over a high-lipped bunker. The low pitch, under these

Photograph 58.

conditions, would cause the ball to roll too far whereas the cut shot will fly high and stop quickly. These two pitching techniques, the low pitch and the high pitch combined, cover a distance from five yards to 60 yards out.

What's next? Inside five yards from the green we will use a very special technique called "bent-arm chipping." This will be covered in our next chapter. From 60 yards to your full swing wedge, which will probably be 90 to 100 yards for an average player, the sequence of club choice is three-quarters, or three-quarter wedge, then one-half swing, 9-iron. Depending on the situation, a full wedge or three-quarter 9-iron, which are somewhat synonymous, would be used next. After this we move through the clubs from short to longer or from the higher numbers to the lower numbers, depending on the distance and always using our full swing. As you recall from an earlier chapter, the full swing clubs will hit a ball approximately 10 yards apart from its neighbor. This is due to different shaft lengths and different degrees of pitch or loft in the clubhead.

Photograph 59.

CHAPTER 15

BENT-ARM CHIPPING

I call this shot, bent-arm chipping, my secret weapon. It is not commonly used by most players as I teach it; however, it is deadly accurate from the edge of the green to five yards out. Its purpose is to clear the longer grass close to the green, land and roll up to the cup. Don't discount the importance of this shot close in as it will improve your game noticeably at the distances mentioned.

Your choice of clubs and gauging of distances is very precise for this shot. At three feet from the edge of the green, use the 5-iron; six feet, the 6-iron; nine feet, the 7-iron; 12 feet, the 8-iron; and 15 feet, the 9-iron. It is easy to remember the progressions as every three feet we change clubs. So we remember three, six, nine, 12, 15 equals the 5, 6, 7, 8 and 9-irons. Or to put it another way, for each three feet of grass we wish to cover or jump over, we need about three degrees of loft change in our clubhead. The landing spot on this shot is one or two feet inside the green. As we begin to explain the mechanics of this shot, our distance or roll to the cup is gotten from the speed with which we move the clubhead.

The stance in the address position is square. The feet are about six inches apart. With the left toe now turned to a parallel position to the right foot, it is no longer turned out slightly as in the full swing. In essence we are standing in a small box with our feet parallel to the sides of the box. The ball is played center in our stance. We take a slight knee bend and bring the knees in so that the weight is inside the feet and toward the heels. Take your grip and slide your hands down the club until the thumb and forefinger of the right hand touch the steel shaft. This position is drastically choked down. The right hand is backed off until it faces the target. The back bend is enough to let our plumb line from the eye to the ground center directly over the ball. Therefore the ball is only about six inches from our foot line, so it's very close in.

The only way we can address the ball at this tight of a position is to raise the club up on its toe. The club stands on its toe and is straight up and down. The right elbow is in against the right side. The left elbow is out and pointing to the target. The left elbow has a very noticeable bend. The hands are moved forward to a position three inches out from the left leg which is the position where our hands are set for all clubs. Our eye line is straight over the ball. This particular plumb line is shown in Photograph 60. It is very important that the club is up on its toe and when we hit the ball it is still on its toe. The club is taken straight back with the shoulders only. There's no head movement, no

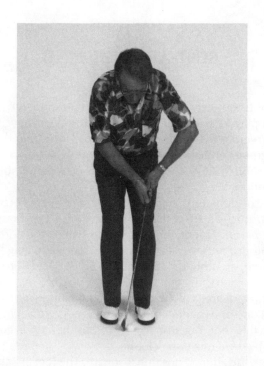

Photograph 60.

leg movement and no wrist-cocking motion. When the club is moved through impact, it goes only as far as the right arm can extend. This is shown in Photograph 61. The hips and legs do not move as the shot is so short that we don't need the extra horse power or mass that we have in the lower body during the bigger swings.

The length of the backswing approximately equals the length of the follow-through. The left wrist and shoulder are welded into position so that the only movements are with the shoulders and the right arm. The stroke is slow and then quick. We take the club back straight along the target line and straight through with a pulling left hand. The tempo of the downswing is approximately twice as fast as the backswing. The toe of the club brushes the grass and the ball pops up and jumps.

As we move through our clubs from the 5 through 9, the loft or pitch to the face increases as we move back from the green. The stroke is the same with all five clubs. The advantages of this type of chip shot includes several things. First, the eye is directly over the ball and the club is swinging in a true pendulum. Second, we only have two moving parts: the shoulders and the right arm. Third, by having the toe of the club on the grass, we don't have any chance to bury the club into a fat shot. If we follow-through with the extended right arm, we will not hit at the ball, but hit through the ball. Fourth, we finish with the club in a very low position, only two or three inches above the ground. Photograph 61 shows the finished position for the bent-arm chip.

Photograph 61.

CHAPTER 16

SAND PLAY

In a standard explosion shot out of a bunker, where the sand is dry, the ball is not contacted by the clubhead. A pad of sand is compressed between the clubhead and ball. The sand iron is the correct club to use. Before getting into this in more detail, the mechanics of the swing must be set up.

The feet are eight to 10 inches apart. The stance is open. The shoulders are parallel to the target line. The target line and foot line are shown in Illustration 3. We open up the stance in order to clear the hips more quickly in the downswing. The ball is played in line with the left heel, or more commonly referred to as off the left heel. This is a change in ball position over the low and high pitch shots where the ball is played center.

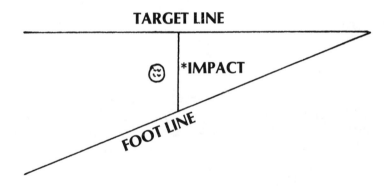

Illustration 3.

As we cannot ground the club in the sand under a two stroke penalty, we must learn to address the ball without touching the sand. This is accomplished by choking down slightly on the club. The club face is open about 30 degrees. This movement helps prevent contacting the sand with the toe of the club first, spinning the clubhead out. The ball will still roll straight as we recall that the sand squeezes the ball from the bunker. The thickness of the pad of sand contacting the ball plus clubhead speed determines how far the ball will travel. The club takes a half-moon shaped cut from under the ball as shown in Illustration 4. The three numbers shown indicate different points of impact. If you learn to take either a one inch, two inch or a three inch pad of sand and control your tempo, you will have three shots at your command

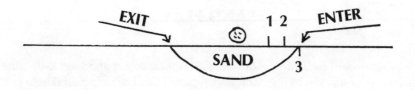

Illustration 4.

with as close a tolerance as can be expected. Practice will teach you how far the ball flies in these three cases.

The stroke is like the high pitch shot, that is, half-swing to half-swing (see again Photographs 58 and 59 on the high pitch shot). The three changes in the sand technique over the high pitch are: open stance, open club face, and ball off the left heel.

The swing is one, two, pause, three, using the same timing sequence as the high pitch. The most important thing to remember is to finish. A major problem is quitting on the swing by hitting at the ball and stopping. A solid, strong, half-finish will get a greater number of balls out of the bunker. Instead of looking at the ball, we look at the point of impact. If you plan a two inch pad of sand, look two inches behind the ball. Set the feet by wiggling them back and forth until the spikes are well-below the top of the sand. This movement also lets you feel the condition of the sand (how hard or how firm), helping you make a decision as to how much sand to take at impact.

There are other conditions you will encounter in a bunker besides soft, dry sand with a decent lie. The first of these is the buried or plugged ball on the face of the trap, possibly near the lip. To make this shot, close the club face drastically, 45 degrees is about right. Hit two inches behind the ball straight into the face of the bunker. The ball will exit easily with an overspin and a straight roll. The left leg will be extremely flexed.

When the sand is wet and hard, your best two choices are putting and the bent-arm chip. A lot of bunkers have less lip and a flatter face toward the side. A putter used to roll the ball out will usually be successful. With a higher lip, the bent-arm chip works well. Select one more lofted club than called for at the basic distance. Use more downswing speed, but only brush the sand with the club at impact. For further distances, the low pitch with a sand iron works well. In all cases the club cannot be grounded prior to impact.

When you're in a fairway trap two changes will be needed. First select one more club. In other words, if it's a 5-iron shot, take a 4-iron. Play the ball back one or two inches in the stance from the normal position used for the particular club you are playing. By moving the ball back slightly you will take less sand at impact. Above all, when playing out of bunkers around the green, keep the hands soft, use a flowing body rhythm and do not quit at the ball. Remember follow-through is the key to good bunker shots.

CHAPTER 17

PUTTING

Putting is similar to bent-arm chipping, except the ball is played in line with the left instep and the club rests flat on its sole. This is the only time that our club is totally flat in a golf swing. In the bent-arm chip, you will recall the club is on its toe and with all other full swing clubs, we try to have the club resting from the center of the sole to the heel of the clubhead.

There are three basic types of putting techniques: wrist putting, tap putting, and shoulder and arm putting. The person who wrist putts, moves the wrists back and forth in a concave/convex position with very little shoulder movement. One of the problems with this type of putting is that it brings us up off the ball if the wrists move in the forward swing too early. Tap putting is a stroke where the clubhead stops at the ball or very soon after impact. This technique can give us trouble as the tendency is either to push or pull the shot. The shoulder and arm technique, which is the one I prefer, swings the shoulder plane only and keeps all other parts of the body locked in place. All three of these techniques are used by professionals; however, the shoulder and arm stoke is used by more professionals.

With putting we have a grip change. It is called the reverse overlap. We accomplish this change by taking the forefinger of the left hand and reversing it or placing it on top of the little finger of the right hand. There are many variations of the putting grip which ultimately becomes a personal thing. But for a person that has not established his grip, start with the reverse overlap as just described.

The stance is square with no turning out of the left foot. The feet are placed approximately 10 inches apart. The knees are in slightly with the weight toward the center and back to the heels of both feet. This is similar to the full swing stance except it is quite a bit more narrow. The weight is equal on both feet. The legs remain locked in their bent position with no movement during the stroke.

We have two options with the left arm. In both cases the elbow is slightly bent. Our first option is to keep the left elbow in fairly close to the left hip. The other option is to point the left elbow to the target as described in the chapter on bent-arm chipping. The right elbow is in close to the right hip. The stroke is straight back and straight through along the target line keeping the club low to the ground. There is no wrist-cocking motion and no movement of the lower body. For the first time, the stroke is even- back and forth- and not the one, two, pause, three, or the slow and quick. By applying an even stroke, we make the ball roll more decisively toward the target. At this point it is a good idea to think or picture the ball rolling to the hole as though you were standing away and watching someone else. By thinking ahead to the hole we mentally visualize the action of the ball before it happens. Photograph 62 shows the putting address position.

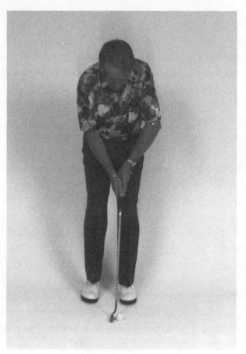

Photograph 62.

There is an exercise that we use in putting which will improve our ability to putt drastically. It is called the chalk-line exercise. Greens are very seldom level as they have a tendency to break from left to right or from right to left. Most hardware stores sell a chalk line which is used in construction. I suggest that you fill your chalk line container with yellow chalk as it shows up the best on green grass. At the end of the chalk line is a hook which we place at the lip of the hole. Moving back a few feet and letting the string in the chalk line out, we then bend down and snap a chalk line on the green. It is best to move around the hole and snap several chalk lines of different lengths and at different positions to the hole. They should look like the spokes of a wheel when you have your chalk lines in place. You then place a ball on one of the lines and say to yourself, "If I hit this ball straight down the line, what is it going to do?" After you mentally decide if it's going to break in one direction or another, you hit the ball straight down the line and watch what happens to it.

As an example, if the ball rolls eight inches to the right of the cup, you correct one-half the distance in the opposite direction. In this case, our correction would be four inches. I call this a one-cup correction. I think in terms of one-cup, two-cup and three-cup corrections. A three-cup correction being 12 inches would take care of a 24 inch break, which is substantial. Hit a ball on your new line which, following this example, would be four inches in the opposite direction and the curve of the green should bring the ball into the hole. Proceed around the circle looking at each chalk line thinking what the ball would do if you hit it straight down the line. Then do that move first and make your corrections second. Do not think, "It breaks six inches to the left; I'll play it three inches to the right." Make sure you hit down the line first, and then see the physical break and apply the correction as just discussed.

This chalk line exercise is the fastest way to become an accurate putter. There's an old saying, "never up, never in." The ideal putt would roll into the cup on its last revolution. I prefer to think slightly past the hole, which will give us a better percentage of shots going in than if we think at the hole. The chalk lines you have snapped on the practice green will disappear overnight, or be washed away by the sprinkler systems, so don't worry about them leaving a permanent mark on the green.

In putting, then, there are three major things to remember. See, in your mind's eye, the ball rolling to the cup. Use an even stroke, and work with an even tempo.

CHAPTER 18

SIDE-HILL LIES

There are four situations that you will encounter which will fall into the category of side-hill lies. These four situations are shown in Illustration 5. When playing with the uphill lie, the left leg must be flexed more in the stance position, otherwise you will have too much weight on the right leg. In order to account for the uphill position by flexing the left leg, you are able to even out your weight, which we are attempting to have equal. Because we will reach the ball late in our swing arc, play the ball two to three inches forward of the normal position for the club that you are using. The hill will make the ball fly higher as if we took a rifle and aimed it more toward the sky instead of parallel to the ground. To account for this higher trajectory, we must take the next lower or longer club. If it is a 5-iron shot, take a 4-iron to lower the trajectory and come out with about the same distance as the hill will elevate the flight of the ball. In this situation the ball will tend to draw from right to left. Therefore, your target line must account for this and be slightly to the right of your intended target. I suggest that you use a slightly shorter backswing.

In the downhill position we are going to reach the ball earlier in the swing arc, therefore, play the ball back in your stance two to three inches from its normal position. The right leg must be flexed more in the downhill lie in order to equalize our weight and keep from shifting too quickly to the left and lunging at the ball. As we are now aiming the rifle into the ground we need to elevate the trajectory or flight of the ball, therefore, take the next higher or more lofted club. In this situation take a 6-iron instead of a 5-iron. Plan for the ball to fade or tail off from left to right; so here we must create a target line left of our target to plan for the fade.

When you find that the ball is above the feet, the weight will tend to be more on the heels and you will feel like you are falling backwards. Therefore, we must place more weight toward the toes to account for the hill on which we are standing. Because the ball is above the feet, you need to choke down on the club, which is best done by placing the club on the ground and sliding the left arm down until it's straight. The ball position is played normally. When the ball is above the feet, plan for a draw. Again, when the ball is going to move from right to left, we must alter our target line slightly to the right to account for this drifting in of the ball toward the target.

When we find ourselves with the ball below the feet, we must place the weight strongly on the heels as the tendency is to fall forward. There are two tips here that may help you on this type of a shot. Because of the slight

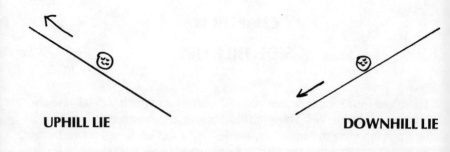

UPHILL LIE   **DOWNHILL LIE**

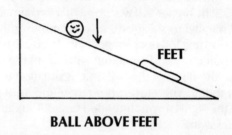

BALL ABOVE FEET

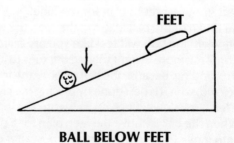

BALL BELOW FEET

Illustration 5.

centrifugal force of the swing, it is suggested that you play the ball more toward the toe of the club. This allows for the slight tendency for the weight to move further out on our toes as we swing at the ball. A second tip is to supinate the wrists strongly because in this situation the ball will fade. To help overcome the left to right direction and the centrifugal force of the swing, play the shot in a direction slightly left of the target to allow the fade at the end of the flight to curve the ball in toward your target. You will run into combinations of these problems where you have a hill which combines two of the situations described, so you must plan to alter accordingly.

Experience is the best teacher in helping you to alter your basic positions of swing, weight, flex and target line. With a little work on these four side-hill lies, they will become more second nature for you without you having to think through each situation. It is advisable if you are a beginner to take four 3 x 5 cards and label them with each of these problem areas. Write out the four or five changes you will make over your basic swing set-up.

Our game has now come to what we hope has been a successful round of golf. Utilizing and improving on the information shared in each chapter throughout this book, each golfer should now have all the components necessary for that consistent golf swing. The individual pieces of the puzzle have fallen gracefully into place presenting a completed picture, a round of golf with scores aiming for the national average, or even below.

Thus we have taken our arsenal of 14 weapons, learned when and how to use them for distance and for placement on the green, and have become that smoothly oiled mechanical person who consistently hits good balls. By concentrating on only one or two chapters in this book, we would be unbalanced; maybe we could hit some terrific distance drives from the tee, but as has been so often said: "but can you score." With the proper grip, by letting the left hand lead, by following that important timing, tempo and rhythm in each part of the swing, we all can score and score lower, which in this game is the same thing as making it big.

NOTES

NOTES

NOTES